> *When dost thou*
> *bring out a lamp*
> ***then*** *to hide it away*
> *beneath bed or bowl?*
>
> *Wouldst thou not first*
> *place it up on a stand*
> *so the flames can be*
> *shared all around?*

JESUS OF NAZARETH

BIRTH of **JESUS** (2024)
comprises 28 chapters
extracted from the volume
BOOK of **JESUS** - A UNIFIED
GOSPEL IN ENGLISH VERSE (2024).
Translation © E. d'Araille, 2021-2024.
First published in limited issue paperback
edition by *LIVING TIME* ™ *Global*, 2024. This
paperback volume © *LIVING TIME* ™ *Books*, 2024.

A CIP (Cataloguing in Publication) Data Record
for this title is available from *The British Library*.

ISBN 978-1-908936-60-8

All images are taken from the original
engravings of Gustave Doré in the
'*Grande Bible de Tours*' (1866).

LIVING TIME ™ *BOOKS*
livingtimebooks.com

BOOK of JESUS

Limited Edition

Special Release #1

~ YESHUA HAMASHIACH ~

JESUS 'THE ANOINTED ONE'

— BORN BETHLEHEM 4 BCE —

BIRTH of JESUS

NATIVITY & ANOINTMENT

from **BOOK** of **JESUS**

A UNIFIED GOSPEL IN ENGLISH VERSE

The One who
*comes **after** me*
*comes **above** me*
because He came
***before** me —*

JOHN THE BAPTIST

Composed by

Edouard d'Araille

and based entirely upon the complete
texts of the four canonical gospels -
of Matthew, Mark, Luke & John

A NOTE UPON CAPITALIZATION

Please take note that in some chapters Jesus of Nazareth has been referred to as 'He', 'Him' *etc.* - with a capitalized 'H' - while in other ones this is not the case. In those instances where such capitalization has occurred, the main reason for doing so has been to place emphasis upon *his person* - especially when another male pronoun has also been utilized in close textual proximity. It is the opinion of the translator that use of such capitalization may dispel confusion in a number of instances. It has **not** been done as an assertion of Jesus' divinity, *which is not a choice for the translator to make.* — Readers are free to interpret the capitalizations in the text however they wish. Christians and non-Christians will naturally tend to approach the text in alternative ways. Use of fully capitalized words has been done on numerous occasions for emphatic or dramatic effect, especially where it is believed that this will clarify the sense of the passage. Please note that the gospel sources are only indicated at the very end of each chapter, the names of the evangels being abbreviated as 'Mt' for Matthew, 'M' for Mark, 'L' for Luke and 'J' for John - followed by chapter and verse reference for the passage or passages forming the basis or the partial basis of that section. -

PAGEFINDER

BIRTH of JESUS

NATIVITY & ANOINTMENT

extracted from **BOOK of JESUS**

A UNIFIED GOSPEL IN ENGLISH VERSE

BEFORE THE BEGINNING

A NEW LIFE

'THE ANOINTED ONE'

PREFATORY NOTE

Book of Jesus is a fully poetized version of the canonical New Testament gospels (Matthew, Mark, Luke & John) composed by contemporary English language poet Edouard d'Araille. It is entirely based on the gospel texts - which were written in Greek - and takes into account every single sentence of every one of the four gospels, channeling all of the incidents and language of the evangelists into a single, unified poetic work. In *Book of Jesus*, all of the events of the gospels are presented in a series of 300 distinct episodes that do not ignore any lexical elements in the sources. The entirety of that translation is appearing in a set of three volumes, releasing from 2025. —

Birth of Jesus, the current publication, is a limited edition select collation of texts from Vol. 1 of *Book of Jesus*, comprising the birth narrative ('nativity') and a series of passages about John the Baptist and Jesus' anointing. The 'Opening Words' and *Prologue* to the first volume are also included as they introduce the first stage of the gospels' narrative perfectly. The main twenty-two chapters of *Birth of Jesus* form a complete chronological sequence, while the four chapters under the heading '*The Anointed One*' narrate a separate and shorter, consecutive progression of events. The volume is closed by a bonus extract from volume one of *Book of Jesus* entitled, "*You Are the Light of the World*" - an example of how inspiring Jesus of Nazareth's words can be:

"Whoever hath ears to hear me - **let them hear** AND UNDERSTAND!"

Algernon P. Smith ANCIENT SCRIPTURES EDITOR - March 21st 2024

BIRTH of JESUS

NATIVITY & ANOINTMENT

"Verily, I say to thee:
thine eyes will behold
the Heavens open -
Angels of God
ascend and
descend -
the SON OF MAN
thine eyes shall see!"

JESUS OF NAZARETH

Composed by

Edouard d'Araille

and based entirely upon the relevant
texts of the four canonical gospels of
Matthew, Mark, Luke & John

To YOU,

O highest

friend of GOD

- Theophilus -

these words

I write. —

(L 1:3)

HOW MANY are the authors

who with words

have writ of

what occurred — of

WHAT HAS BEEN FULFILLED?

Verses that were passed down

to us — what eyes beheld

which TESTIFIED

AS SERVANTS OF

THE WORD.

In the steps of YOUR *servants*

I take up my pen and with words

delve back, on those moments reflect;

I strive to describe the events in order

*that **You** may know the* REAL TRUTH

— of all that has been learned.

(L 1:1-4)

*The LIGHT doth shine
in Darkness
and
by Darkness
it shall not be drowned!*

Prologus

ANTE OMNIA*

BEFORE
All Else
existed,

L o g o s
W A S

- the Word
which WAS
with GOD

and which
itself
WAS **GOD**.

Even since
the Birth
of Time

HE WAS
w i t h
GOD.

* 'Before Everything'

Through HIM,
a COSMOS
came
to Being -

without
HIM,
NOTHING
would become

— for HE
was L I F E,
illuminating
All who live.

The LIGHT doth shine

in Darkness

and

by Darkness

it shall not be drowned!

A man
named John
by GOD was sent

to testify about
that Light.

He came
as witness
to the Truth
so
through him
ALL MIGHT
BELIEVE.

This man
was not himself
the LIGHT

but came
as witness to it -

a dawning Light

now shines

upon

the World,

THAT ALL MAY SEE.

Through HIM,
a COSMOS
came
to Being -

without
HIM,
NOTHING
would become.

His being
grew up in
this World

yet although
He had come
from this World,

it did not know Him.

Unto this Earth
He came - His
Own World
- *but **by this
World, He was
barely welcomed.***

Yet
to those
who received
Him and

those
who believed
in His Holy Name,

**he granted the right
to be** CHILDREN
OF GOD -

children
not birthed
from a woman's
womb, nor by
will of man

- nor by
human
choice.

*His
children
were born
of GOD
alone.*

THE

WORD

BECAME

FLESH and

He founded

His House

among us.

We
have
opened
our eyes to
His GLORY —

Pure Glory of a

Unique and

Solitary

Son.

He
came from
the Father to us,

filled with Grace,

lit up by
Truth.

John, when
he spoke of Him,
testified thus:

*"for Here is
the One whom
I spoke of in
saying:*

**'The One who

comes after me

comes above me

because He came

before me.' — "**

Out

of his

PLENITUDE,

all receive *grace*

- in the place

of GOD's

grace,

which was

granted already.

The *Law* - as we know

- it comes via Moses

yet Grace and Truth

are through Jesus

= THE CHRIST =

No human eyes

have *seen*

GOD

ever

for ONLY

the unique,

the solitary

One - who

is His Son

and GOD

Himself *in*

union bound

— *REVEALS HIM.*

(J 1:1-18)

BEFORE THE BEGINNING

*Devoid of form
was all — a Void —*

*FACE OF NIGHT was
upon the Abyss*

GENESIS 1:2

1. THE VISION OF ZECHARIAH

WHILE HEROD,
as King, ruled
in all of Judea,
Zechariah lived

— of the priestly
division of Abijah,
wed to *Elzbieta,**
of Aaron's line.

Before God,
they were both
so pure - in His
eyes *so righteous*;

all His Laws
they honored —
commands obeyed —
of all blame they were free.

But alas, of offspring
they were bereft.

* 'Elzbieta' - Elizabeth

- Elizabeth was
barren, she could
not conceive - both
her husband and she
so far gone in their years
yet no child had they still.

One day, while his order
performed sacred rites,
he was chosen at
random - as custom
dictates - holy incense to
burn in the House of God.

— Zechariah, he entered
the Temple of *YAHWEH*,
the hour approached that
the censer be lighted;

outside a congregation,
throngs awaited —
together were
joined in prayer.

That instant appeared
unto Zechariah
an angel of the Lord,
standing right beside him;

there, *at the right of*
the altar - where
fragrance was burning -
HE looked straight at him.

The priest was unsettled
*- **a fear** chilled his soul -*

yet the angel then spoke
to him, in these words:

"*Freeze not in terror,*
dear Zechariah —
thy SUPPLICATIONS,
they have been heard.

Elizabeth - thy spouse -
shall bear a son to thee
and thou shalt call him
by the name of 'JOHN'.

The *Joy of Life* shall
HE be to you both and
to many HIS BIRTH — **it
shall bring jubilation**.

In the sight of the Lord
HE WILL HAVE GLORY
- nor liquor nor wine
will he ever imbibe;

'fore even this child
is out of the womb
- HIS SOUL IS INFUSED
WITH THE HOLY SPIRIT.

How many of Israel's
children shall **this one**
turn unto the Lord
— their God! —

To them he will
go with the soul
and the might of
ELIJAH before him.

Hearts of parents,
so hardened to Love, to
their children shall return;

those who have
disobeyed the Lord - ***to***
the wisdom of HIS JUSTICE.

His actions will make
the people ready
for the LORD.*"*

Yet old Zechariah,
he voiced only
doubts, and
disbelief —

"Of each word
that you say,
how can I be
so sure? *- For*
my body is ageing
and also my wife is
advanced in her years."

Then to these words
did the angel respond:

"*GABRIEL am I*
- in the presence
of God I stand and
to you have been sent
to share SUCH GOOD NEWS.

From this moment forth,
THOU SHALT MAKE NOT
A SOUND — IN FACT
THOU WILT NOT SPEAK
TILL THE DAY THAT ALL THIS
HAS COME TO PASS - *for thou*
didst not believe my words;

in good time, you will
see, **they shall be**
proven TRUE."

While this happened,
the people outside who
were waiting ask: "*Why doth*
he bide in the temple so long?"

Yet when he emerged,
Zechariah SPOKE NOT
- people *sensed* he had
witnessed a vision inside.

He continued to beckon
to them with signs **but**
he could not utter
a single word. —

As soon as his duties had
been fulfilled,
the priest returned
to his home -

after that day
did Elizabeth duly
conceive - and five months
she remained all alone, thinking:

"*Thus hath the* LORD
acted - **pitying me** *- in*
removing the shame that
had darkened my name."

(L 1:5-25)

2. THE BETROTHED

HERE FOLLOWETH
how those events
came to pass, that
the birth of *JESUS -
MESSIAH* - occurred:

The mother of Jesus,
named Mary, was
promised to Joseph who
from David hailed

— yet even before
they were joined as
one, she was found
to be pregnant - *by
the* **Spirit***'s power.*

Joseph, faithful
to the LAW - and
not desirous of public
disgrace - was minded
to break off from
his betrothal.

*   *   *   *   *   *

At that time
Elzbieta, with John,
was now six months
progressed *when*

God sent to Earth
GABRIEL - *angel* -
to Nazareth,
Galilee. —

He sent HIM to
Mary - *the virgin* -
whom Joseph had
pledged to wed.

(Mt 1:18-19 / L 1:26-27)

3. A VIRGIN'S VISITATION

WHEN GABRIEL
came unto Mary,
he said to her:

*"Greetings to thee -
thou who art so
highly blessed
among women —
the Lord is **with thee**."*

At these words
of the angel
was Mary
perturbed —
wondering quite
what the greeting meant.

However, he carried
on saying to her:

*"Be thou not afraid,
O MARY,
full favor hast
thou found with God.
A baby in thy womb shalt
thou conceive and to
this son give birth,
and name HIM
as 'JESUS'.*

— *Upon THEE,
the HOLY SPIRIT
shall descend*

Great will He be
and He shall be called
The Son of the One Most High.

To Him, Lord God
shall present the throne
of David, His father on Earth

— over Jacob's sons and
daughters, He will rule
for ever more —
His Kingdom never die."

"But how can this be,"
Mary said to the angel,
 "since I have never
   lain with man?"

To which Gabriel
answered,
saying:

"Upon thee
the Holy Spirit
shall descend; the might
of the Lord on High shall cast
His shadow upon **thee** *- thus*
the Sacred One shall be
born, to be known as
the 'Son of God'."

Then the angel
continued:

"Elizabeth, thy kin,
herself will bear a child -
she who now is agèd and
has been called **barren** *-*
already today, she is
six months gone —

No Word of God
shall ever fail
to grow."

"Handmaiden
of the Lord am I,"

responded Mary:

"Let every word
that THOU *hast*
said, **thus** *be*
FULFILLED."

And at
that point
the angel left.

(L 1:27-38)

4. THE FIRST DREAM OF JOSEPH

AFTER JOSEPH
had dwelt on
these things
in his thoughts,

unto **him** came
an angel (the LORD's)
whilst dreaming,
and said to him:

"Joseph - son of
David's House -
Fear not *to make*
Mary thy wife, to
bring her inside
thy home. For
that which is
inside her womb
takes its life from
the HOLY SPIRIT.

A son, of Mary,
shall be born and
His name, IT SHALL BE
'JESUS' — *for His nation*
He brings from their
sins unto ***Salvation.***"

(Mt 1:20-21)

5. A PROPHET'S WORDS FULFILLED

THUS DID
all this come to pass
that the words spake by God
through His prophet
should wholly be
fulfilled:

"For

the Virgin

will then become

pregnant

and

then shall

give birth to a son

and to him

will

be

given

the name

'IMMANUEL'

— 'God with Us'."

(Mt 1:22-23)

6. 'AS THE LORD COMMANDS'

THUS
when Joseph
awakened, he did
what the Lord had
demanded
of him.

Mary
he took in
his house as
his spouse,
yet
their union
would not be
consummated
till *after* the birth
of their **son** - and
to him he gave
the name
of 'JESUS'.

(Mt 1:24-25)

7. "BLESSÈD ART THOU"

THEN IT WAS
Mary made ready
and went with great haste
to a town in the hills
of Judea —

here did she
enter a home,
Zechariah's —
his wife Elizabeth
greeting her there.

The instant Elizabeth
heard Mary's voice
speak, the baby
leapt round in
her womb —

she was filled
with the Holy Spirit

— in voice
firm and strong
she proclaimed
unto Mary:

"— Blessèd art THOU
of all women and blessèd
the fruit that thy womb
shall bear.

Tell me, —
why am I so blessed
that the **Mother of the** LORD
should come hither
to visit me?

— No sooner
than thou camest
near and the sound
of thy greeting was heard
in my ears - **then**
the infant leapt joyous
> *within me.*

— Blessèd is she who
has fully believed that
the Lord would make good
on those promises that
He had made to us!"

(L 1:39-45)

8. THE SONG OF MARY

MARY THEN
proclaimed:

*"My soul sings its
glories to the* LORD,
*for my spirit rejoices
in all its joy, O GOD
- **O** MY **SALVATION***!

*— For HE has
attended to one who
is modest in being
HIS* SERVANT.

*From this day forth,
all times and peoples
shall name me* **'blessèd'**
for what GOD ALMIGHTY
performed through me.

*Hallowed be **His Name**
— His Mercy reaches even
those who fear Him — from
one generation to the next.*

— *With His arms alone*
He has mastered great feats;
those with naught but pride
in their innermost thoughts,
He has soon dispersed.

Kings has He thrown
from their thrones yet
the humble and meek -
He has hoisted on high.

Those who were famished,
He fed with His nourishment;
affluent ones He sent back to
their homes - empty-handed.

Israel, His servant, hath He
helped in many ways,
so mindful of her in
*His **mercy** - to our*
fathers, Abraham
and his descendants,
forever, as was pledged."

(L 1:46-55)

9. 'HIS NAME IS JOHN'

THREE MONTHS LONG
Mary stayed with
her cousin, then
headed home. -

The day came
and Elzbieta
gave birth to
her son then
her kith and kin,
hearing quite how
the Lord God had
shown **her** such mercy
- *they joined her in joy.*

When the eighth day
arrived, it was time for
the boy to be cleansed —

he was just then about to
be called 'Zechariah'
like father,
the same.

However, on hearing
these words, Elizabeth
said: "*That **cannot** be so -
for his name must be 'John'.*"

"*What do you mean?*"
they responded:

"***Not one of your
blood** EVER
bore that name!*"

— Those assembled
made signs to the father
to know what he wanted
to name his own son.

He motioned to them
for a writing tablet, then
shocked them all writing
'***Let 'JOHN' be his name***'.

Immediately, IN
THAT SELF-SAME INSTANT —
Zechariah's mouth was opened,
his tongue could speak again
AND **GOD** HE PRAISED.

His neighbors, each
one overwhelmed
with awe - over
all of the hills
of Judea
spread word of
what happened there.

— Every person
who heard about
John exclaimed:

"*What FATE*
*can **such** a*
child have?"

FOR THE HAND
OF THE LORD
WAS UPON
HIS LIFE.

(L 1:56-66)

10. THE SONG OF ZECHARIAH

INSTILLED WITH
the Holy Spirit,
Zechariah spake
in prophecies:

*"God of Israel, **praise**
be to Thee,
O LORD —
for He hath
come down
to His people,
He hath offered
them REDEMPTION.*

*Our LORD holds
a Savior's bugle
aloft in the land
of HIS servants -
in David's House*

*— as foretold
by His prophets,
before it took place.*

We **have** been delivered
from our foes - **and**
from the blades of
those who hate us.

We **must** extend
the MERCY that was
promised to our forebears
and **honor** the PLEDGE that
had been sworn to our
father - ABRAHAM:

that we, being
rescued from our
enemies' clutches, will
do our Lord's bidding,
AND FREE OF ALL FEAR —

in sanctity and purity
live before Him
each day of our lives!

O THOU, dearest son,
shalt be called
the 'PROPHET
OF GOD ON HIGH';

thou wilt go into
the presence
of the Lord —
prepare the path
  = for HIM =

Thou wilt make
His people know
REDEMPTION - **how**
all can be freed
from their sins.

— Only through
the tender mercies
of our God, through
whom the dawning
Sun rises to waken us,
wilt Thou illumine those
who dwell in the darkness
and in the shadow of death.

Thou guidest
our feet upon the path
that leadeth

       unto PEACE."

(L 1:67-79)

A NEW LIFE

*Once the basket was open
she gazed on the **infant**.*

Behold! — it wept, and
SHE HAD **LOVE** FOR IT*!*

11. **A CENSUS FOR CÆSAR**

IN THOSE DAYS
Augustus Cæsar
did publicly order
that stock should be
taken of whom Rome
could tax: a *Census of
the Roman Empire* -
the first as Cirenius
governed in Syria.

Thus did everyone
go to their home town
to sign themselves
up to be taxed. —

And so Joseph,
among them, left
Galilee's Nazareth,
going Judea-bound
- Bethlehem - whence
he descended from
David's House.

Thither
he travelled
with Mary, to
register them
for the taxes.

At that point - in
marital union bound -
Joseph's wife now was
approaching the end
of her pregnancy.

(L 2:1-5)

12. IN THE TOWN OF DAVID

DURING THE DAYS
they were there
in Bethlehem,
birth was due.
When the time
came, a boy unto
Mary was born —
their first-born son.

First he was wrapped
up in swaddling cloths,
then placed down beside
them, in manger of stone;

for
there
was no
guest-room
available here, so
they had to make do
with the animals'
quarters, a stable
to keep them
safe and
sound.

Out in the fields
close by, shepherds
lived, who were watching
their flocks by the light
of the moon —

at that point there

appeareth an angel

to them, of the Lord's,

and the light of Divinity

shone and illumined

the space all around

*- **and they gasped***

***in sheer marvel**.*

The angel,
it said,
reassuringly
then:

"*BE YE ALL*

NOT IN FEAR,

For I bring you

GOOD NEWS *that*

will make all your

people UNITE

IN JOY.

For on this day,
in David's town,
THE SAVIOUR has
been born to you -
Anointed One *and*
long-awaited **Lord.**

— And let this be
a sign for you – a baby
bound up in its swaddling
cloths within a manger
YOU SHALL FIND."

And at that very instant,
multitudes of angels
stood around
the one who spoke
- all giving praise to God,

announcing:

"Glory be unto GOD
in Heaven on High
and on Earth — let
Peace reign upon those
whom HE ***justly favors.***

Once the angels of God
had returned to
the Heavens,
the shepherds
spoke straightway
amongst themselves:

" — *We must*

make our way

to Bethlehem —

WITNESS all that

the Lord God

has told us

about."

(L 2:6-15)

13. **SHEPHERDS PAY HOMAGE**

SO THEN
all the shepherds
departed, soon finding
both Mary and Joseph
— with Jesus in
manger.

- The moment
that they laid their
eyes on *this child*,
all of them started
to share
the GOOD NEWS

— and each one

who heard them

was stunned by

the words that

the shepherds

were speaking.

- *the shepherds departed,
soon finding both Mary and
Joseph — with Jesus
in manger*

Meanwhile
Mary delighted
at all that occurred
then - *so special* - she
thought on it deep
in her heart.

And the shepherds
went back to their flocks,
praising God in His Glory
for all they had seen
and heard, —

which had been
just exactly
as they
were forewarned.

(L 2:16-20)

14. "WHERE IS THE NEW KING?"

AND AFTER WHEN
Jesus was born
in Judea —
in Bethlehem,
while Herod
was King,

a group of Magi
from Eastern lands
arrivèd then in
Jerusalem.

Of Herod
they asked:

*"O where is the
newly born 'KING
OF THE JEWS' ?*

*We have followed
His star **hence**
we come here
to worship HIM.—"*

Instantly Herod
had heard what
was said **then**
his head set in
turmoil - *and
all of the City.*

Herod called
chief priests and
teachers of Law - to
stand there before him -
to answer him clear: "***Where
then - this Holy 'Messiah' -
is He to be born?***"

They replied right away:
"*Bethlehem - in Judea*",
for all of them knew
the Prophet's words:

"*Yet ye, in Bethlehem
- Land of Judah - are
by no means the most
modest in that land, for
thence comes a Monarch
— **for Israel, their Shepherd.**"*

We have followed His star
hence we come here
to worship HIM

And after that
Herod convened all
three Magi *clandestinely* -

precisely learning from
them when HIS STAR
began to shine.

To David's town
he sent them,
saying:

" *— Go there and*

search ye cautiously

- then, once you find

him, send word back

that I may come

to HONOR HIM."

(Mt 2:1-8)

15. THREE MAGI BRING TRIBUTES

ON HEARING ALL
that Herod bade,
the wise men went
upon their way, —

following the risen star
until it led where
HE was born.

Arriving in that place,
the Magi
all exulted finding
HIM.

Stepping within,
they could see
the new baby
- *behold it* -
together with
Mary, its mother;

they bowed down
at once, to pay
HIM tribute.

Then with

their offerings

each one approached

HIM - with treasures

of **gold** and of

frankincense,

myrhh.

*   *   *   *   *   *

The Magi
were shown
in a dream that
they must not return
to King Herod again

*- they **paid heed** to*
that warning
and made
their way back
by a different route

AT ONCE.

(Mt 2:9-12)

16. A TIME FOR PURIFICATION

THEN, ON
the eighth day
past he was born,
- the time came to
make the boy pure
in God's eyes,

— he was
christened
as 'JESUS' just
as was foretold
by the angel before
his conception.

- After that,
Mary his mother,
went also through rites
of purification —
imposed by
the laws of Moses.

Joseph and Mary,
with Jesus, then
went to Jerusalem,

there to present him to
GOD - as is also laid
down in the Law:

"*For every*
first-born male,
unto the LORD *he shall*
be consecrated."

They went there
as well to give
presents of
sacrifice,

owing to that
which is writ:

"*Give a couple of*
doves or a pair
of young pigeons."

(L 2:21-24)

17. **SIMEON'S BLESSING**

IN THAT TIME
Simeon dwelt
in the City
- one so
righteous,
pious, devout;

the HOLY SPIRIT, it
rested on him while
awaiting Israel's
consolation.

To Simeon
the SPIRIT spoke
- *reminding him **he
would not die till God's**
'MESSIAH' HAD REVEALED
His *face to him.*

Animated by
this thought,
he went toward
the Temple Court

— *there* were
Mary and Joseph
with Jesus, in keeping
with custom, to get
the boy blessed.

Simeon then held
the child in his arms
and with words of praise
he prayed to God, saying:

*"Lord Supreme, as
Thou hast promised,
I, Thy servant, may
now be dismissed —*

*at peace – for presently
mine eyes have witnessed
Thy Salvation, One that
THOU hast made for
EVERY NATION*

*— A **light** for
the enlightenment
of non-believers **and** for
Glorious Splendor of
Thy People, **Israel**."*

Every word that
they were told,
the child's parents
heard in awe. —

And after that did
Simeon his blessing
on the boy bestow,
and blessing TO
THEM ALL and
to his mother
Mary; **then
he said**:

*"Your infant son,
the Fates divine,
shall be the cause
of Rise and Fall in
our nation - Israel -
a SIGN against whom
many, they shall fight.*

LET INMOST THOUGHTS

OF MANY HEARTS BE LAID

OUT BARE - FOR THAT WOULD I

SUFFER A SWORD PIERCE MY SOUL!"

(L 2:25-35)

18. ANNA, THE PROPHETESS

AT THE TEMPLE
dwelled also
a *prophetess*
who was
named Anna;
daughter of Penuel
- Asher's tribe.

Ancient in years
was this soothsayer,
seven years only with
husband, a widow -
now *eighty-four*.

— But not one time
ever did Anna depart
from the temple —
she prayed there,
she worshipped,
she fasted - *all*
day and all
night.

At that instant,

>she came up to

Mary and Joseph;

>she told them how

due to their child,

>she made deepest

praise to the Lord.

And Anna

>spoke openly,

happy to

>talk of this boy

who was

>'*HE LONG-AWAITED -*

THE PEOPLE'S REDEMPTION'.

(L 2:36-38)

19. A DREAM OF EGYPT

SOON AFTER THE MAGI
had come to worship
Jesus and departed,

an angel of the Lord again
appeared to Joseph
in a dream —

"Quick, get up
and leave!"
it told him -
"Begone with
your child and
his mother - - -
flee to Egypt *NOW!"*

And after that,
the angel added:

"I warn you, **not**
to move from there
until the day I tell you,
– BEWARE, for Herod, he
is hell-bent on finding
your son to KILL HIM!"

(Mt 2:13)

20. HEROD'S VENOM

ON REALIZING
they had fled
without returning
to him - Herod was
enraged at how
the Magi **so** had
mocked him.

Out of fury,
Herod ordered
all those boys of
two and under *to*
be slaughtered —
those who resided
near Bethlehem.

He did this due to
knowing what the three
wise men had taught him

- and **thus,**
that spake by Jeremiah
came to be
fulfilled:

*— Rachel crying for
her children, shunning
every word of comfort,
- she shall find no solace*

"In Ramah,

I hear voices

weeping, wails

of LAMENTATION

— Rachel crying for

her children, shunning

every word of comfort,

- she shall find no solace

for her boys are dead

and gone, NO MORE.*"*

(Mt 2:16-18)

21. A DREAM IN EGYPT

AFTER THE COUNSEL
the Lord's angel
gave him -
Joseph departed
with mother and child

- Bethlehem leaving
beneath cloak of night,
they set on their path
toward Egypt's land.

And there they resided,
as family — just
until after the life of
King Herod had passed.

Thus, yet again,
were the words that
the Lord spake through
prophets come true:

"For out of Egypt,
I have called
my Son."

Joseph departed
with mother and child
- Bethlehem leaving
beneath cloak of night

After Herod
expired, again
did an angel of God
come to Joseph, to give
him this warning:

*"Go, take your family,
wife and son with you,*
RETURN NOW TO ISRAEL —

those who had sought thy

*child's life **have gone**."*

(Mt 2:14-15; 19-20)

22. 'A NAZARENE'

— SO JOSEPH THEN LEFT
and went back with his wife
and their son to Israel.

However, on hearing
that, after
his death,
Archeläus
now reigned
in King Herod's place

- **he froze with fear.**

After the vision he saw
in his dream,
Joseph moved them
to Galilee —

and there they dwelled
and made their home
*the town of **Nazareth**.*

So thus were fulfilled
the prophet's words:

*"He shall be called a **Nazarene**."*

- Joseph and Mary
had done all that God
wished and followed
the Law when they
lived out in Egypt.

Nazareth, hometown,
where they would all live
— there the child, he grew,
both in body and wisdom;

the **Grace** *of* **God**

WAS UPON HIM.

(Mt 2:21-23 / L 2:39-40)

' THE ANOINTED ONE '

Touch Not
My Anointed Ones
— unto my Prophets
DO NO HARM

PSALMS 105:15

THE WORD OF GOD

THE SON OF
Zechariah grew —
in spirit strong became.

*In the reign of Tiberius -
Year 15 - while Judea
was governed by
Pontius Pilate,*

*while Herod the Tetrarch
in Galilee reigned and
his brother,
King Philip,
Iturea and Traconitis
ruled - Lysanias,
monarch of
Abilene,*

*during
the priesthood
of Annas and
Caiaphas. —*

Then

was when

John heard

God's Word in

in the wilderness;

waiting to preach

to the people

of Israel

- he lived

in the desert

until it was time.

Then

he appeared

on the banks of

the Jordan:

teaching,

baptizing —

redeeming from sins.

(L 1:80; 3:1-3)

"MAKE READY THE WAY"

A DAY
of Good News
has now dawned
upon us

of Jesus
- the Christ -
the Anointed One;

for the SON OF GOD,

as foretold by Isaiah:

'I send Thee a herald
to light Thy road.

Dost Thou hear
the voice of one
who calls out from
the desolate plains? -

"Make ready the way
of the LORD, - for
His paths you must
make straight!" '

*Dost Thou hear
the voice of one
who calls out from
the desolate plains?*

Thus did the Baptist emerge
from the wilderness:
JOHN, who would preach
the forgiveness of sins.

In the waters he purged
the hearts of sinners,
christening all in
repentance come.

All   of
Judea
and
all of Jerusalem

came out to find him,

professing their sins -

in the river of Jordan

their souls were

redeemed

through

the power

of God's absolution.

"Repent! The Kingdom
of Heaven is nigh! —"

announces the voice of
this man from the wild:

"Each valley is filled,
each mount abased,
the crooked is straight
and rough now smooth

— all of you people
I bring the **news** *—*
GOD's Advent of
SALVATION!"

In raiments knit
from hair of camel
- a band of leather
around his waist -

surviving on locusts
and honeys of nature,
John, on the Jordan,
baptized *every day.*

To Bethabara they
came in their hordes,
holy leaders come also
to meet with John —

Pharisees,
Sadducees,
Levites and more,
from Jerusalem, all
had this question
for him:
"WHO ART THOU?"

Straight away did John,
of his own will, confess:

*"— I'm not the 'Messiah',
I am not* **The One.***"*

*"Then are you Elijah?
or Are you the Prophet?"*

To each of these queries
did John respond, *"No"*.

In total frustration they
asked him: *"Then WHO?
We must bring back
an answer to those
who have sent us!*

- **Who do you say
that you** REALLY ARE*?"*

Instead of
his own words,
John quoted Isaiah:

*"Mine is
whose voice cries
aloud from the wilderness:*

**'Make straight
the path for the Lord!'"**

*   *   *   *

Now some Pharisees
who had been sent
there expressly,
re-questioned
him now in
a different way:

"If you're no 'Messiah'
**- then
why the anointing?**

If you're no Elijah,
**then why
do you
speak like
the Prophet thus?"**

Stepping forth toward
crowds who
awaited
anointing,
John spake to
the Pharisees,
Sadducees - *words*
with flames ablazing:

"*Ye nest of vipers!*
- who warned ye to
flee from the wrath
yet to come?! —

Produce the fruit
of repentance,
not sentences
hollow and numb!

— Do not start off
by telling yourselves,
so entitled: 'ABRAHAM,
HE IS OUR FATHER ALONE

- WE CAN DO NO WRONG - '

For I tell ye that
out of these stones themselves
God can fashion
new children for him!"

For the blade of the axe
is struck hard
at the roots

- every tree
that produces
bad fruit is hacked
down and consigned to

the

FLAMES!"

   *   *   *   *

"Then what should we do?"

asked the masses
there gathered,

and John spoke
to all of the people thus:

"Whoever hath two shirts
*- **give one who has none***

and

whoever hath food, **share**
with those - without!"

Collectors of taxes
came there too for
baptism, quizzing John:

"*What must we also do?*"

- He replied: "*Do not
take one bit more than
you're meant to —
tax only the money
that's truly due!*"

Even soldiers were
stood there
and also
called out
to him: "*John,
tell us, what must we do?*"

To whom he responded:

" *- Do not coerce money
when that is extortion.*

*Do not bear false witness
where none are to blame*

— and Finally, **be thou
content with your pay!**"

People on all hands
were waiting
expectantly,

many were
wondering:

"Is He the CHRIST*?"*

John   could
sense all of their
questioning hearts,
so he stood up and
answered the
populace
thus:

"I am the one who baptizes
with WATER, *that all*
may repent of
their sins

but after
comes One far
more mighty than I
Who baptizes with FIRE

and   the   HOLY   SPIRIT

— In your midst steps
the One in whose presence
I dwindle, the straps of whose
shoes I'm not fit to undo -

nay, whose sandals
I'm not even
worthy to
hold!

See, in His hand
is a harvesting fork,
to separate out all
the grain from
the chaff -

with this
does He clear
the threshing floor -

storing wheat in His barns

as unstoppable fires
burn husks
to ash - "

With these
and with other words
John unveiled all the GOOD NEWS
he had learned to his brethren there —

(M 1:1-8 / Mt 3:1-12 / L 3:4-18 / J 1:19-28)

'THE LAMB OF GOD'

AND AT
THAT TIME
Jesus of Nazareth
came up the banks of
the Jordan - from Galilee.

When
John saw
Him walking
towards him, he
uttered these words:

"Behold -

the Lamb of God,
He who cleanses ALL SIN
from the World —

Here is the One
Whom I meant
when I said:

'The One who
comes after me
comes above me
because He came
before me.' —"

But when
Jesus arrived
before John
in person,

the Baptist
immediately
said to Him
this:
*"It is I
and not You
who have
need of
anointing
- yet YOU
come to
me?"*

"Yes I do,"

answered Jesus:

"that's how it must be

**for only in this way will
each act of God's plan
be reached with
perfection".**

John no longer
deterred Him and
promptly complied.

"*It is I and not You who have need of anointing - yet YOU come to me?*"

- Thus
was Jesus
baptized
by John in
the Jordan - who
afterward spoke of
what happened like this:

"At the moment
He rose from
the waters,
the heavens above
opened   *wide.*

What I saw

was

the

SPIRIT

of

GOD

coming

down

in

the

form

of

a dove

- on His forehead
it rests.

*He
looked
to the skies
in prayer as it
sat there — a voice
from above spake forth:*

*'I AM WELL PLEASED
WITH YOU -
MY SON*

*- WITH YOU
WHOM I LOVE'."*

Then
John, he
reflected:

*"Before we had met
here I never had known*

HIM.

*For **what reason** had I
'The Baptist' become*

*— than **anoint**
the 'MESSIAH'
for our Holy
Land?-"*

After, John
spoke to many
of what he had seen:

*"I myself did not know Him
but HE who first sent me
to baptize with water,
HE told me before -*

*'When you
WITNESS
the SPIRIT
d e s c e n d
upon Him
- KNOW HE
IS THE ONE
who baptizes
with SPIRIT'*

- I SAW WITH

MY EYES

AND I TESTIFY

HERE -

THAT THIS WAS

IN TRUTH

GOD's

UNIQUE

CHOSEN ONE."

(M 1:9-11 / Mt 3:13-17 / L 3:21-22 / J 1:29-34)

FOLLOWERS OF JESUS

THE SUCCEEDING MORN
again,
John was there and
he
pointed out Jesus
to
two of his followers:

*"There, don't you see,
HE who passes —
the Lamb of God?"*

On hearing this,
both of them
went after Jesus
and followed behind;

noticing them,
He turned round
and He asked them:

"What do you want?"
and they bowed,
saying: *"Rabbi...*

*O teacher, just tell us
please, where are
you staying?"*

"Come hither,
I'll show you",
to them He replied

- so they went
right along and saw
where He was lodged,

and they spent
the whole day with
Him, till it was dusk.

Andrew - the brother
of Simon - was
one of the two who
had heard what John said;

after following Jesus,
he sought out his brother
to tell him: *"Dear Simon,*
the CHRIST *has been found!"*

And once he had found him,
he brought him to Jesus,
who looked in his eyes and
said:
    "Simon, **hear me**
- son of John - I'll call
you now '**Cephas**',
Peter, the Rock."

Jesus,
the next day,
He made a decision
to make His way to Galilee.

Leaving,
He met up with
Philip and said to him:

"*COME NOW AND FOLLOW ME.*"

Like Peter and Andrew,
he came from
Bethsaida,

on finding Nathanael,
he shared what
he knew:

"*At last*

we have found

He whom Moses

has written of, —

One of whom also

the Prophets spake:

Jesus of Nazareth -

Joseph's son."

"From Nazareth!
What good e'er hailed
from there?!"

On hearing
his harsh exclamation
did Jesus
step close to Nathanael,
saying:

"In truth, stands
an Israelite
here
in whom
lies no deceit. — "

"But how do
you know me?"
said he, turned to Jesus:

"There I observed you,
sitting 'neath
the fig tree's shade,
then Philip called you."

Nathanael spoke aloud,
proclaiming:
"KING OF ISRAEL
ART THOU, RABBI - **SON OF GOD!"**

To which
Jesus answered:

"Though you believe
since I told you of
how I knew you
before we met -

TRULY SHALT THOU
WITNESS THINGS
FAR GREATER —
MORE AWESOME
THAN WORDS CAN SAY."

Then He concluded:

"Verily, I say to thee:

thine eyes will behold

the Heavens open -

Angels of God

ascend and

descend -

the SON OF MAN

thine eyes shall see!"

(J 1:35-51)

"YOU ARE THE LIGHT OF THE WORLD"

THEN HE SAID TO THEM:

*"When dost thou
bring out a lamp
then to hide it away
beneath bed or bowl?*

*Wouldst thou not first
place it up on a stand
so the flames can be
shared all around? -*

*That which was hidden
is meant to be* SEEN —
*the **concealed** now
placed in the* LIGHT OF DAY.

*— What was closed off
from our sight **is to**
be disclosed -
in your eyes now*
NEW REVELATIONS.

*Whoever hath ears
to hear me —
let them hear*
AND UNDERSTAND!"

After saying all this,
Jesus added:

"Ponder long on
what you hear —
about its meaning
think at length:

as much
as you give
will be given
*to you **and far***
greater besides

for WHOEVER
MORE POSSESSETH,
SHALL BE GIVEN MORE,

while those
who haveth not,
*lo, **the little they have***
will be taken away
from them - ALL
SHALL BE LOST!"

Detecting that
clouds of confusion
persisted, Jesus
went on, saying:

"YOU ARE THE LIGHT
OF THE WORLD, I say,
like a town on a hill
you are witnessed by all
- and never can fail
to be noticed!

Just as none
light a lamp
to entrap in
a jar of clay -

no, *that lamp*
is placed up on
its stand so that
all in the house from
its flames RECEIVE LIGHT -

likewise, I say
LET THY LIGHT SHINE FORTH
FOR ALL - so that
others may see your acts
of goodness -
and so they may glorify
YOU —
OUR FATHER IN HEAVEN."

(M 4:21-25 / Mt 5:14-16 / L 8:16-18)

What was closed off
from our sight **is to be
disclosed** - *in your eyes*
now NEW REVELATIONS

TRANSLATION & RESEARCH

ACKNOWLEDGEMENTS

In such an abbreviated form as this, it is only possible to faintly hint towards the many debts of knowledge that are owed to an extremely wide range of texts and authors: the best-preserved source texts in the original *Koine Greek*, in excess of fifty New Testament translations of the Bible gospels, the non-canonical gospels (helpful to issues of chronology and in other ways), the body of 'Gospel Harmonies' that have been produced since the *Diatesseron* of Tatian (2nd Century ACE) *and* the absolutely overwhelming wealth of scriptural scholarship that has amassed over nearly two millennia since the gospels first appeared. The voices of Irenaeus, St. Augustine and Thomas Aquinas, of Friedrich Schleiermacher, Søren Kierkegaard, Albert Schweitzer, William Barclay, Karl Barth, Gerd Lüdemann and William Lane Craig - these few represent only the tiniest chorus of those whose researches on translation, interpretation *et al.* have been considered during the convergence of the four gospel texts into a unified poetic work, however perilous may be the performance of such a task. - Regarding the present publication, which provides the entire combined nativity sequence of the four gospels and the sequence of John the Baptist anointing Jesus, questions of the historicity of events have been a guiding focus of research and composition. As a glimpse of Jesus of Nazareth's charismatic eloquence, experienced by the reader continually throughout the gospel texts, an extract from the chapter entitled *"You Are the Light of the World"* has been featured at the close of this volume. It is only the hope of the composer of this translation that it will bring inspiration to those who peruse it.

Edouard d'Araille - February 29th 2024

Published by

This Publication is set in
Gloucester MT Extra Condensed and
Adobe Devangarari

Whoever does EVIL
despises the LIGHT *and*
*evades its glare for **fear***
their deeds will be exposed;

but those who live their lives
through TRUTH *shall enter*
in the LIGHT, *that all may*
see what they have done
within the EYES *of* GOD.

JESUS OF NAZARETH

www.ingramcontent.com/pod-product-compliance
Lightning Source LLC
Chambersburg PA
CBHW060949050726
47592CB00003B/1171